RABBITS, RABBITS & MORE RABBITS!

By GAIL GIBBONS

HOLIDAY HOUSE · New York

FOR DIANE FOOTE

Special thanks to Amy Cook, D.V.M.
of Stonecliff Animal Clinic, Bradford, Vermont

Copyright © 2000 by Gail Gibbons
All rights reserved
Printed in the United States of America
First Edition

Library of Congress Cataloging-in-Publication Data

Gibbons, Gail.
Rabbits, rabbits, & more rabbits!/by Gail Gibbons.—1st ed.
        p.   cm.
SUMMARY: Describes different kinds of rabbits, their
physical characteristics, behavior, where they live,
and how to take care of them.
ISBN 0-8234-1486-8
1.   Rabbits Juvenile literature.[1. Rabbits.] I. Title.
SF453.2.G53   2000
636.9'32—dc21
99-16765
CIP

DALMATION
REX

FLEMISH
GIANT

SIAMESE
DWARF

There are wild rabbits and tame rabbits. Tame rabbits can be gentle and loving pets.

A FOSSIL is the hardened remains or traces of plant or animal life preserved in rock.

The first rabbits lived about 65 million years ago. Their fossils have been found in China and Mongolia. In North America the oldest fossils are about 37 million years old. Ancient rabbits looked a lot like today's rabbits.

ALL MAMMALS are warm-blooded animals, and their babies are born alive instead of being hatched from eggs.

HARE

TEETH, called INCISORS

RABBIT

Rabbits are members of the leporid family along with their close relatives, hares. All hares are wild. Leporids have two rows of sharp front teeth used for gnawing. They are mammals.

COTTONTAIL RABBIT

EUROPEAN COMMON RABBIT

The two most common kinds of wild rabbits are cottontail rabbits and European common rabbits. Wild rabbits live on every continent except Antarctica. All tame rabbits are descendents of European common rabbits.

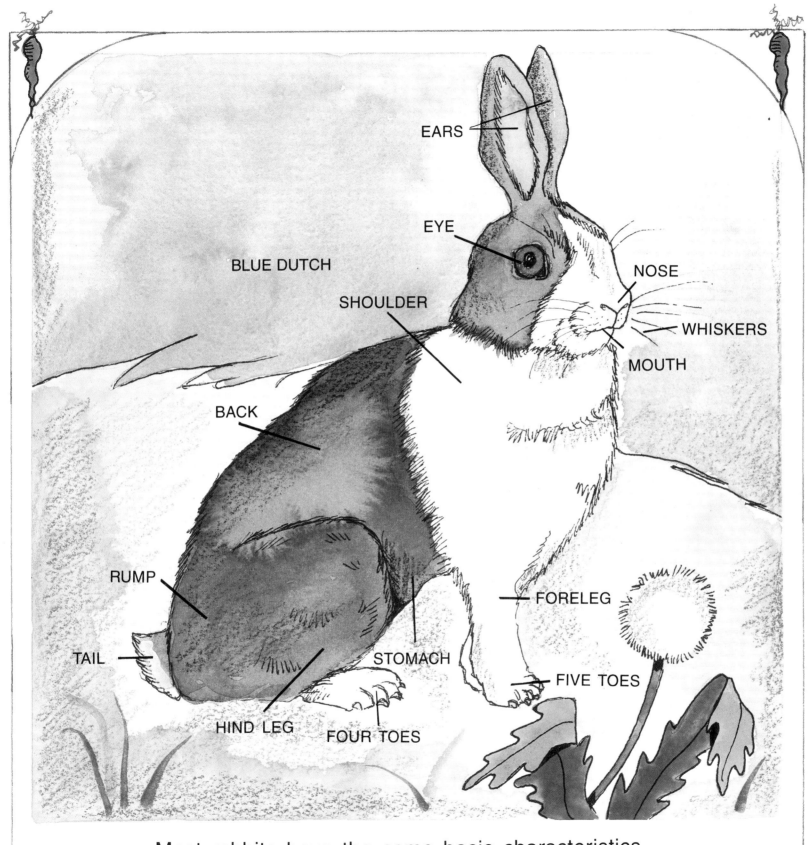

EARS

EYE

NOSE

WHISKERS

BLUE DUTCH

SHOULDER

MOUTH

BACK

RUMP

FORELEG

TAIL

STOMACH

FIVE TOES

HIND LEG

FOUR TOES

Most rabbits have the same basic characteristics.

There are big rabbits and small rabbits. Their heads can be pointed and narrow or broad and flat. Wild rabbits have short brownish fur. Domestic rabbits have short or long fur that can be white, black, gray, reddish, brown or a mixture of these colors. Their fur keeps them warm.

Most of the time the short, fluffy tail of a rabbit has a splash of white on it. When a rabbit senses danger, it will flash the white of its tail as a warning to other rabbits.

Hop…hop…hop! Rabbits get around by using their powerful hind legs. They can also run as fast as 18 miles (29 kilometers) an hour. Many can leap 10 feet (3 meters) or more.

Pads of soft, spongy fur under its feet protect the rabbit's toes. These pads also give the rabbit a good grip as it leaps or runs. Often, when a rabbit senses danger it thumps a hind leg on the ground as a warning to other rabbits.

A rabbit depends most of all on its excellent hearing. It moves its ears together or one at a time to catch the sounds coming from any direction.

Rabbits can see better in the dark than people. A rabbit's eyes are on the sides of its head. Because of this, it can see to both sides as well as to the front and back. A rabbit has a good sense of smell, too. Its nose wiggles constantly as it sniffs to identify any scents.

Rabbits that live in the wild have all kinds of enemies. They are hunted by foxes, hawks and many other animals. Their biggest enemy is people who hunt them for food and for their fur.

When an enemy appears, a rabbit may stay very still to not be noticed. Or it may run away.

Rabbits are vegetarians. That means they don't eat meat. In the spring and summer months, wild rabbits eat leafy plants. Biting and chewing helps wear down their front teeth, which grow continuously. During the winter months, they live on bark twigs and the old fruit of bushes and trees.

FORM

BURROW TUNNEL

A WARREN is a series of underground burrows and tunnels.

Cottontail rabbits nest and sleep in a shallow hole called a form. During the winter, they find protection under brush, wood or in the shelter of a ledge. The European common rabbits live in warrens dug by the female rabbits.

Rabbits are nocturnal. They eat and play most of the night from dusk to dawn. During the day they rest and sleep.

A well-cared-for pet rabbit can live eight to twelve years. In the wild a rabbit may live to be about five years old. A male rabbit is called a buck. A female rabbit is called a doe.

KITS also
called KITTENS

The doe cottontail rabbit carries her young inside her body for about thirty days. Several times a year she will give birth to four to eight babies in a group called a litter. Baby rabbits are called kits or kittens.

They are born with their eyes closed and without any fur. To keep them warm the mother covers them with grass and bits of her fur in the form, or nest, she has dug in the ground. At about a week old, the kits have opened their eyes and grown a coat of soft fur.

When they are about two weeks old, the kits leave their nest. They dig their own forms. Their mother only nurses them for the first few weeks of their lives. Then they begin to find their own food.

When they are about six months old they begin to raise their own young.

RHINELANDER

A domestic kit is old enough to leave its mother when it is about eight weeks old. It's fun to adopt a baby rabbit or a grown rabbit for your own pet, but you must allow time to take care of it.

HOW TO TAKE CARE OF YOUR RABBIT
There are about 50 breeds of domestic rabbits.

Handle your rabbit gently and speak softly. Never pick up a rabbit by its ears. When holding a rabbit, grasp its hind legs for support.

Your rabbit needs a place to call its own. Usually this is a rabbit cage.

A special water bottle should be hung on the side of the cage. Change the water daily.

Feed your rabbit dried rabbit food twice a day. Feed it one handful of greens, vegetables and fruit once each day, too. Rabbits love carrots. No rhubarb allowed! A rabbit loves a salt lick, too.

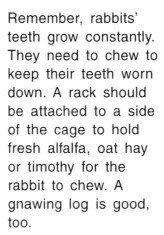

Remember, rabbits' teeth grow constantly. They need to chew to keep their teeth worn down. A rack should be attached to a side of the cage to hold fresh alfalfa, oat hay or timothy for the rabbit to chew. A gnawing log is good, too.

Keep your rabbit's litter box clean.

Your rabbit needs to exercise outside its cage for at least 30 minutes a day. Never leave it alone when it is outside its cage.

Keep your rabbit clean and well groomed.

Give your rabbit safe toys for fun and exercise.

Take your rabbit to the veterinarian for its yearly checkups.

Always remember... your rabbit needs love and care.

CARING FOR AN INDOOR PET RABBIT

Your rabbit needs a cage to call its home and to sleep in. The cage needs to be big enough for your rabbit to stretch out.

Keep your rabbit's litter box in a place your rabbit can get to easily. Always keep it clean.

Line the cage with wood shavings. Change these often to keep the cage clean.

NEVER let your rabbit chew on electrical wires!

Many people keep their rabbits as indoor pets.

CARING FOR AN OUTDOOR PET RABBIT

HUTCH

A hutch must have lots of space for your rabbit to live in.

Put the hutch in a safe place away from any other animals.

Keep the hutch in the shade, away from bright sunlight.

If the hutch doesn't have a wire bottom, cover the floor with wood shavings. Put a nest box inside the hutch. Put hay inside the nest box so your rabbit can make a bed. Clean the hutch out often.

When it is very cold outside bring the hutch inside to a warm and protected area.

Other people build outdoor homes for their rabbits, called hutches.

CINNAMON CHINCHILLA

Often, people enter their pet rabbit in shows or contests. Sometimes these are held at fairs. The rabbit that is judged to be the best wins.

TORTOISESHELL DUTCH

WHITE DWARF

NEW ZEALAND RED

Rabbits are lots of fun to watch in their natural environment. But, best of all, rabbits are fun to play with. They are wonderful pets that require lots of care, attention and love.

THE DIFFERENCE BETWEEN A WILD RABBIT

A WILD RABBIT

A NEWBORN RABBIT
HAS NO FUR.

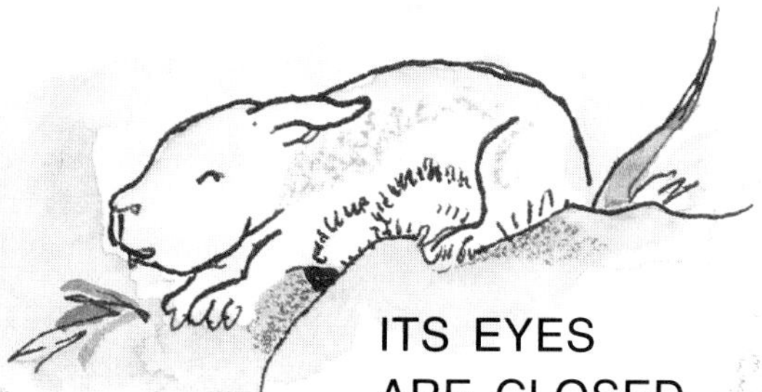

ITS EYES
ARE CLOSED.

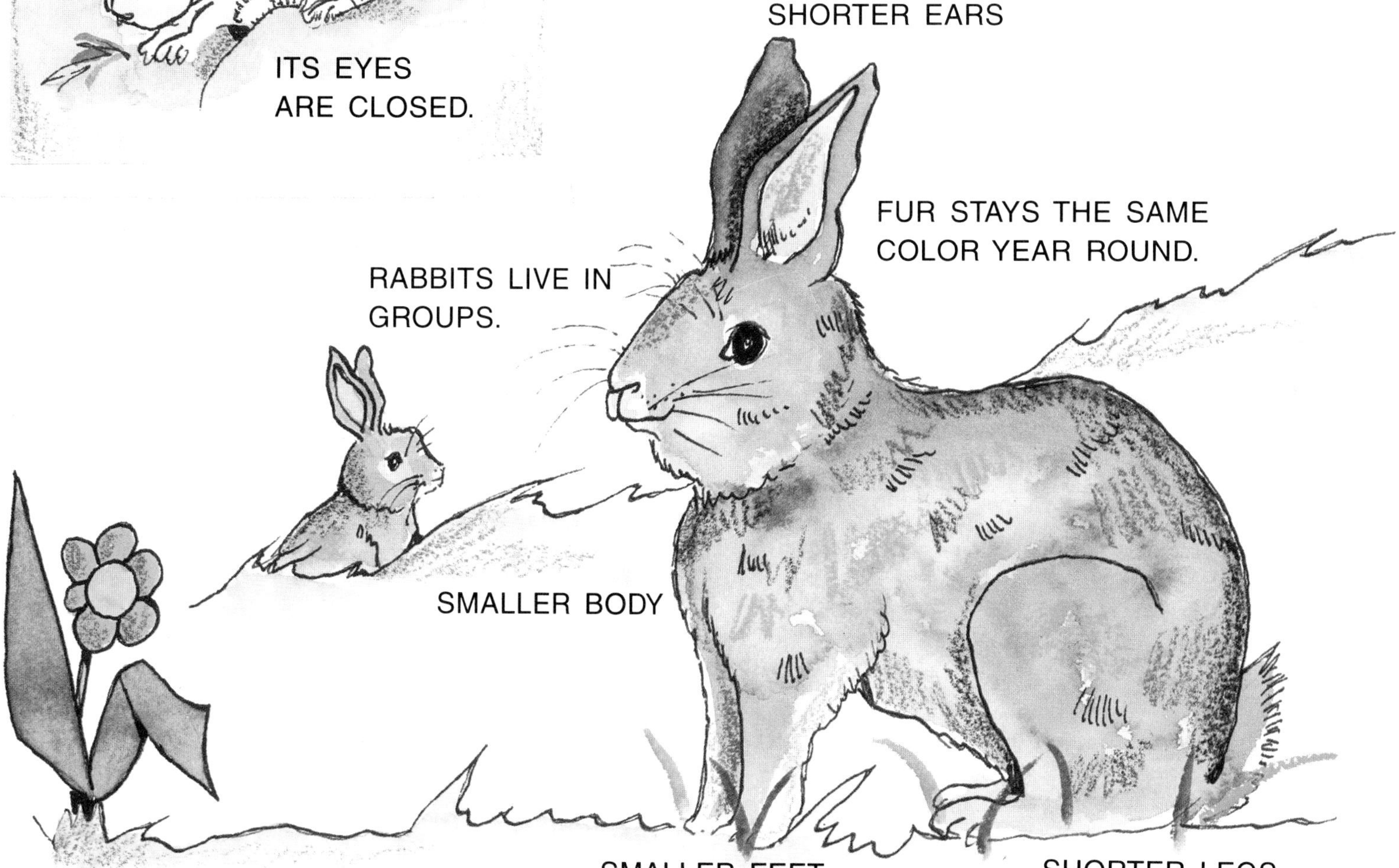

SHORTER EARS
FUR STAYS THE SAME
COLOR YEAR ROUND.
RABBITS LIVE IN
GROUPS.
SMALLER BODY
SMALLER FEET
SHORTER LEGS

A HARE

A NEWBORN HARE HAS FUR.

ITS EYES
ARE OPEN.

LONGER EARS

SOMETIMES FUR
TURNS WHITE DURING
WINTER.

HARES LIVE ALONE.

BIGGER BODY

BIGGER FEET

LONGER LEGS

NEVER try to tame a wild rabbit.

A jackrabbit is a kind of hare. It can run as fast as 45 miles (72 kilometers) an hour.

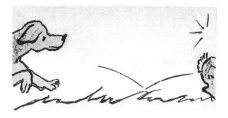

When a rabbit is very scared it can make a terrible screaming sound.

All wild rabbits' ears stand straight up. Some rabbits' ears hang down. They are called lop-eared rabbits.

The Easter Bunny is probably the most famous legendary rabbit. A German legend tells how the Goddess of Spring turned a bird into a rabbit. The rabbit was able to lay brightly colored eggs. The goddess gave them to children as gifts. That's why we say the Easter Bunny brings eggs.

Most rabbits have dark brown eyes. Pure white rabbits have red eyes.

One of the most famous rabbit stories is "The Tale of Peter Rabbit" by Beatrix Potter.

The smallest kind of tame rabbit is the Netherlands dwarf rabbit. It weighs about two pounds (1 kilogram).

In China it is a tradition that each year is ruled by one of twelve different animals. One of these animals is the rabbit.

The biggest kind of tame rabbit is the Flemish giant. It can weigh about 24 pounds (11 kilograms).

There are millions and millions of rabbits throughout the world.